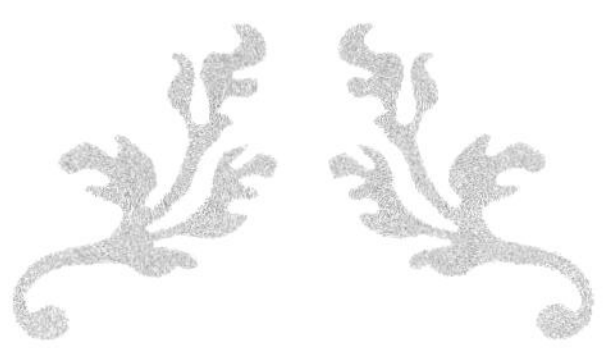

99 DUAs

FOR SUCCESS, HEALTH & SPRITUAL GROWTH

ISLAMIC SUPPLICATIONS FOR DAILY LIFE

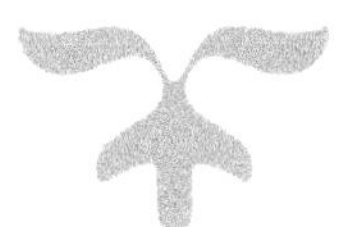

SALAH MOUJAHED
salah@muslimnotebooks.com

CONTENTS

PREFACE

وعن النعمان بن بشير رضي الله عنه، عن النبي صلى الله عليه وسلم

قال: "الدعاء هو العبادة"

ibn Bashir reported that the Prophet, may Allah bless him and grant him peace, said, "Supplication is worship." [Abū Dawūd Rīyāḍ aṣ-Ṣāliḥīn 1465]

The term Du'ā (arabic ٱلدُّعَاءُ) has various meanings in the Arabic language: Worship, seeking help, asking, supplicating, and calling. That is, du'ā is used in different ways to connect one's heart with God and to approach Allah (SWT). Usually, du'ā is a request to God to ask for His help to make one's life easier.

And Allah (SWT) even loves it when we ask Him for something and are persistent in doing so.

وَإِذَا سَأَلَكَ عِبَادِي عَنِّي فَإِنِّي قَرِيبٌ أُجِيبُ دَعْوَةَ الدَّاعِ إِذَا دَعَانِ فَلْيَسْتَجِيبُوا لِي وَلْيُؤْمِنُوا بِي لَعَلَّهُمْ يَرْشُدُونَ

"And when My servants question you about Me, I am near; I hear the call of the caller when he calls on Me. Therefore, let them listen to Me and believe in Me. Perhaps they will take the right path."

[Surah al-Baqarah 2:186]

Prophet Muḥammad (ﷺ) said that there are three ways when one receives the answer to a duʿā:

1. one receives the answer or the result of the duʿā immediately in his life.

2. the duʿā is saved for a later, as yet unknown time in one's life.

3. one receives the answer or the result of the duʿā in the next life (Akhirah).

At the same time, we should always keep in mind that we do not practice duʿās just to get something. Rather, the real goal is to approach Allah (SWT) in this way.

In order for a duʿā to be accepted by Allah (SWT), we should always have positive thoughts when practicing a duʿā. It is also recommended to perform ablution (wuḍu) before a duʿā.

Many Islamic scholars also recommend saying the following words before and after a duʿā:

اللَّهُمَّ صَلِّ عَلَىٰ مُحَمَّدٍ وَعَلَىٰ آلِ مُحَمَّدٍ كَمَا صَلَّيْتَ عَلَىٰ إِبْرَاهِيْمَ وَعَلَىٰ آلِ إِبْرَاهِيْمَ وَبَارِكْ عَلَىٰ مُحَمَّدٍ وَعَلَىٰ آلِ مُحَمَّدٍ كَمَا بَارَكْتَ عَلَىٰ إِبْرَاهِيْمَ وَعَلَىٰ آلِ إِبْرَاهِيْمَ فِي الْعَالَمِينَ إِنَّكَ حَمِيْدٌ مَجِيْدٌ

Allāhumma ṣalli ʿalā Muḥammadin wa ʿalā Āali Muḥammad(in), kamā ṣallaīyta ʿalā Ibrāhīma wa ʿalā Āali Ibrāhīm(a), innaka Ḥamīdun Majīd. Allāhumma bārik ʿalā Muḥammadin wa ʿalā Āali Muḥammad(in), kamā bārakta ʿalā Ibrāhīma wa ʿalā Āali Ibrāhīm(a), innaka Ḥamīdun Majīd.

Translation: "O Allah, send prayers upon Muhammad and upon the family of Muhammad, just as You sent prayers upon Abraham and upon the family of Abraham. Verily, You are the Praised One, the Glorious One. O Allah, bless Muhammad and the family of Muhammad as You blessed Abraham and the family of Abraham. Verily, You are the Praised, the Glorious."

The more du'ās we practice, the closer we are to Allah. In this collection, you will find 99 carefully selected du'ās that are relatively short, memorable, and suitable for everyday use so that we can stay connected to Allah (swt) even in the midst of our daily challenges. By focusing on our connection with Allah (swt), we can cultivate mindfulness and discipline our minds to get our worries and fears under control.

Enjoy reading and reciting the following 99 du'ās. May Allah acknowledge our prayers!

Salah Moujahed

01. DU'A FOR MOTIVATION AND GRATITUDE

رَبِّ أَوْزِعْنِي أَنْ أَشْكُرَ نِعْمَتَكَ الَّتِي أَنْعَمْتَ عَلَيَّ وَعَلَىٰ وَالِدَيَّ وَأَنْ أَعْمَلَ صَالِحًا تَرْضَاهُ وَأَدْخِلْنِي بِرَحْمَتِكَ فِي عِبَادِكَ الصَّالِحِينَ

Transliteration:

Rabbi āuwz'anī an ashkura ni'matikal-latī an'amta 'alaīyyah wa 'ala wālidaīyyah wa an 'āmala ṣāliḥān tarḍhāhu wa adkhilnī bi-raḥmatika fī 'ībādik aṣ-ṣāliḥīn

Translation:

O Lord, direct me to be thankful for the blessings you have bestowed upon me and upon my parents, and to do good works that please You. And admit me, by Your grace, into the company of Your virtuous servants.

Source: Surah An-Naml, 27:19

02. DU'A AFTER WAKING UP

اللَّهُمَّ بِكَ أَصْبَحْنَا، وَبِكَ أَمْسَيْنَا، وَبِكَ نَحْيَا، وَبِكَ نَمُوتُ، وَإِلَيْكَ النُّشُورُ.

Transliteration:

Allāhumma bika aṣbaḥnā wa-bika amsaīnā, wa-bika naḥyā, wa-bika namūtu wa-ilaīyka an-nūshur.

Translation:

O Allah, by Your permission we have reached the morning and by Your permission we have reached the evening, by Your permission we live and we die. And with You is our resurrection.

Source: Jām'i at-Tirmidhī 5:466

03. DU'A AFTER GETTING UP

اللَّهُمَّ إِنِّي أَصْبَحْتُ أُشْهِدُكَ وَأُشْهِدُ حَمَلَةَ عَرْشِكَ، وَمَلَائِكَتَكَ وَجَمِيعَ خَلْقِكَ، أَنَّكَ أَنْتَ اللَّهُ لَا إِلَهَ إِلَّا أَنْتَ وَحْدَكَ لَا شَرِيكَ لَكَ، وَأَنَّ مُحَمَّداً عَبْدُكَ وَرَسُولُكَ

Transliteration:

Allāhumma innī aṣbaḥtu ushhiduka, wa-ushhidu ḥamalata 'Aarshika, wa-malā'īkataka, wa-jamī' khalqika, innaka ant-allāhu lā ilaha illā anta, waḥdaka lā sharīka laka, wa-anna Muḥammadan 'Abdūka wa-rasūluk.

Translation:

O Allah, verily I have reached the morning and I call upon You, the bearers of Your throne, Your angels and all Your creation to testify that You are Allah; that no one has the right to be worshipped except You alone; that You have no partner and that Muhammad is Your servant and messenger.

Source: Abū Dawūd 4:317

04. DU'A FOR SUCCESS IN ALL DOING

اللَّهُمَّ إِنِّي أَعُوذُ بِكَ مِنْ مُنْكَرَاتِ الأَخْلَاقَ، وَالأَعْمَال، وَالأَهْوَاء

Transliteration:

Allāhumma innī a'ūdhu-bika min munkarāt-il akhlāq, wal-'āmāl, wal-ahwa'

Translation:

O Allah! I seek refuge in You from undesirable behavior, deeds and aspirations.

Source: Jām'i at-Tirmidhī

05. DU'A FOR PATIENCE

رَبَّنَا أَفْرِغْ عَلَيْنَا صَبْراً وَتَوَفَّنَا مُسْلِمِينَ

Transliteration:

Rabbanā afrigh 'ālaīnā ṣabran wa-tawaffanā Muslimīn

Translation:

O Lord! Shower us with patience and let us die as Muslims.

Source: Surah Al-A'raf , 7:126

06. DU'A FOR A HEALTHY BODY

اللَّهُمَّ عافِني في بَدَنـي ، اللَّهُمَّ عافِني في سَمْـعي ، اللَّهُمَّ عافِني في
، بَصَـري ، لا إلهَ إلاّ أَنْـتَ .اللَّهُمَّ إنّي أَعـوذُبِكَ مِنَ الْكُفـر ، وَالفَقْر
وَأَعـوذُبِكَ مِنْ عَذابِ القَبْر ، لا إلهَ إلاّ أَنْـتَ

Transliteration:

Allāhumma 'āfinī fī badanī, Allāhumma 'āfinī fī sam'ī, Allāhumma 'āfinī fī baṣarī, lā 'ilaaha 'illā anta. Allāhumma innī a'ūdhu bika min al-kufri, wal-faqri, wa a'ūdhu bika min 'ādhāb-il-qabri, lā 'ilaaha 'illā anta.

Translation:

O Allah, make my body healthy. O Allah, preserve my hearing. O Allah, preserve my sight. There is no one worthy of worship except You. O Allah, I seek refuge in You from disbelief and poverty, and I seek refuge in You from the punishment of the grave. There is no one worthy of worship except You.

Source: Abu Dawūd 5090

07. DU'A WHEN ENTERING A RESTROOM

. بِسْمِ اللَّهِ. اللَّهُمَّ إِنِّي أَعُوذُ بِكَ مِنَ الْخُبْثِ وَالْخَبَائِثِ .

Transliteration:

Bismillāhi allāhumma innī a'ūdu bika min-al-khūbthi wal-khabāith.

Translation:

(In the name of Allah) O Allah, I seek refuge in You from all evil and all evildoers.

Source: Al-Bukhārī 1/45 ; Ṣaḥiḥ Muslim 1/283

08. DU'A FOR CONFIDENCE AND BEFORE A SPEECH

رَبِّ اشْرَحْ لِي صَدْرِي وَيَسِّرْ لِي أَمْرِي وَاحْلُلْ عُقْدَةً مِّن لِّسَانِي يَفْقَهُوا قَوْلِي

Transliteration:

Rabb-ishraḥ lī ṣadrī, wa-yassir lī amrī, wa-ḥlul 'ūqdatan mi-lisānī yafqahu qauwlī

Translation:

O Lord, lift up my heart And ease my task for me, And untie the knot from my tongue, that they can understand my speech.

Source: Surah Ṭa-Ha, 20:25-28

09. DU'A FOR MERCY TO THE PARENTS

رَّبِّ ارْحَمْهُمَا كَمَا رَبَّيَانِي صَغِيرًا

Transliteration:

Rabbir-ḥam-humā kamā rabba-yanī saghīran

Translation:

O Lord! Have mercy on them as they brought me up when I was a child.

Source: Surah Al-Isrā', 17:24

10. DU'A FOR FORGIVENESS FOR THE PARENTS AND GUESTS

رَّبِّ اغْفِرْ لِي وَلِوَالِدَيَّ وَلِمَن دَخَلَ بَيْتِيَ مُؤْمِنًا وَلِلْمُؤْمِنِينَ وَٱلْمُؤْمِنَٰتِ

Transliteration:

Rabbi-ighfirlī wali-wāli-dayya wa-liman dakhala baīytīa mu'minan wa-lil-mu'minīna wal-mu'mināt

Translation:

My Lord! Forgive me and my parents and the one who enters my house in faith, and all believing men and women.

Source: Surah Nuḥ 71:28

11. DU'A FOR RELIEF FROM DEBTS

اللَّهُـمَّ اكْفِـني بِحَلالِكَ عَنْ حَـرامِـك، وَأَغْنِـني بِفَضْـلِكِ عَمَّـنْ سِـواك

Transliteration:

Allāhumma akfinī bi-ḥalālika 'an ḥarāmika wa-aghninī bi-faḍlika 'amman siwāka

Translation:

O Allah, content me with what You have permitted instead of what You have forbidden, and make me independent of all others except You.

Source: Jām'i at-Tirmidhī 3563

12. DU'A TO INCREASE THE PHYSICAL AND SPIRITUAL RESERVES (RIZQ)

اللَّهُمَّ إِنِّي أَسْأَلُكَ عِلْماً نَافِعاً، وَرِزْقاً طَيِّباً، وَعَمَلاً مُتَقَبَّلاً

Transliteration:

Allāhumma innī as-aluka 'ilmān nāfi'an, wa-rizqan ṭayyīban, wa-'amalan mutaqabbalan

Translation:

O Allah, I ask You for knowledge that is beneficial, for good provision, and for deeds that are accepted.

Source: Sunan Ibn Mājah 925

13. DU'A FOR FORGIVENESS

رَبِّ اغْفِرْ لِي رَبِّ اغْفِرْ لِي

Transliteration:

Rabb-ighfir lī, Rabb-ighfir lī

Translation:

Lord, forgive me. My Lord, forgive me.

Source: Sunan An-Nasā'ī 1146, 1666 Abu Dawūd 874

14. DU'A IN STRESSFUL SITUATIONS

اللَّهُمَّ إِنِّي أَسْأَلُكَ مِنْ فَضْلِكَ

Transliteration:

Allāhumma innī as-aluka min faḍlika

Translation:

O Allah, I ask for Your favor.

Source: Abu Dawūd 465

15. DU'A FOR LIBERATION FROM FEARS AND PEACE IN THE HEART

اللَّهُمَّ اكْفِنِيهِمْ بِماَ شِئْتَ

Transliteration:

Allāhumma akfinīhim bimāa shi'ta.

Translation:

O Allah, suffice (i.e. protect) me against them according to Your will.

Source: Ṣaḥiḥ Muslim 4:2300

16. DU'A FOR PROTECTION FROM ENEMIES

اللهم إنا نجعلك في نحورهم و نعوذ بك من شرورهم

Transliteration:

Allāhumma inna naj'aluka fī nuḥurihim wa na-a'ūdhu bika min shururihim.

Translation:

O Allah, I place You before them and seek refuge in You from their evils.

Source: Abu Dawūd 3/42

17. DU'A TO RECOGNIZE THE TRUTH

رَبَّنَا لَا تُزِغْ قُلُوْبَنَا بَعْدَ اِذْ هَدَيْتَنَا وَ هبْ لَنَا مِنْ لَّدُنْكَ رَحْمَةً اِنَّكَ اَنْتَ الْوَهَابُ

Transliteration:

Rabbanā Lā Tuzigh Qūlubānah Ba'da idh ḥadaīytānah wa-habb lanā mil-ladūnka raḥmah innaka anta'l wahāb

Translation:

Our Lord, do not cause our hearts to swerve after You have guided us, and bestow on us mercy from Your presence; You are the Giver.

Source: Surah Āl-'Imrān, 3:8

18. DU'A FOR BLESSING FOR HIMSELF AND HIS FAMILY

رَبَّنَا اغْفِرْ لِي وَلِوَالِدَيَّ وَلِلْمُؤْمِنِينَ يَوْمَ يَقُومُ الْحِسَابُ

Transliteration:

Rabbanā aghfir lī wali-wāli-daīyya wa-lil-mu'mināna yauma yaqūmu alḥisābu.

Translation:

Our Lord, forgive me, and my parents, and the believers, on the Day the Reckoning takes place.

Source: Surah Ibrāhīm, 14:41

19. DU'A FOR STRENGTHENING THE HEART (FAITH)

يَا مُقَلِّبَ الْقُلُوبِ ثَبِّتْ قَلْبِي عَلَى دِينِكَ

Transliteration:

Yā Mūqallib al-qulūbi, thabbit qalbī 'alā dīnika

Translation:

O transformer of hearts, bind my heart firmly to your religion.

Source: Jām'i at-Tirmidhī 3522

20. DU'A FOR A SUCCESSFUL LIFE

اللَّهُمَّ أَصْلِحْ لِي دِينِي الَّذِي هُوَ عِصْمَةُ أَمْرِي ، وَأَصْلِحْ لِي دُنْيَايَ الَّتِي فِيهَا مَعَاشِي، وَأَصْلِحْ لِي آخِرَتِي الَّتِي فِيهَا مَعَادِي وَاجْعَلِ الْحَيَاةَ زِيَادَةً لِي فِي كُلِّ خَيْرٍ وَاجْعَلِ الْمَوْتَ رَاحَةً لِي مِنْ كُلِّ شَرٍّ

Transliteration:

Allāhumma aṣliḥ lī dīnī al-ladhī hua 'iṣmatu 'amrī , wa-aṣliḥ lī dūnīya-ya al-latī fīha mā'shī , wa-aṣliḥ lī ākhiratī al-latī fīha m'ādaī wa-j'al al-ḥaīyāta zīyādatan lī fī kuli khaīyrin wa-j'al al-mauwta rāḥatan lī min kuli sharin

Translation:

O Allah, establish for me my religion, which is the protection of my affairs, and establish for me my world, in which is my sustenance, and my life. Make good of my life after death where I am destined. And make life a complement to me in all good, and death a consolation to me from all evil.

Source: Ṣaḥiḥ Muslim Book 17, Ḥadīth 1472

21. DU'A FOR HEALING

للَّهُمَّ إِنِّي أَعُوذُ بِكَ مِنْ شَرِّ سَمْعِي، وَمِنْ شَرِّ بَصَرِي، وَمِنْ شَرِّ لِسَانِي
وَمِنْ شَرِّ قَلْبِي، وَمِنْ شَرِّ مَنِيّي

Transliteration:

Allāhumma innī a'ūdhu bika min shari sam'ī, wa-min shari baṣarī, wa-min shari lisānī, wa-min shari qalbī, wa-min shari manīyīye

Translation:

O Allah, I seek refuge in You from the evil of my hearing and from the evil of my seeing and from the evil of my tongue and from the evil of my heart and from the evil of my deed.

Source: Jām'i at-Tirmidhī 5/523

22. DU'A FOR STRENGTHENING OF FAITH

رَبِّ اجْعَلْنِيْ مُقِيْمَ الصَّلَاةِ وَمِنْ ذُرِّيَّتِيْ رَبَّنَا وَتَقَبَّلْ دُعَاۤءِ

Transliteration:

Rabbi j'alnī mūqima aṣ-ṣalāti wa-min dhurrrīyatī rabbanā wa-taqabbal du'ā

Translation:

My Lord, help me and my children to pray. Our Lord! accept my supplication.

Source: Surah Ibrāhīm, 14:40

23. DU'A FOR CLEANSING THE SOUL

رَبَّنَا ظَلَمْنَا أَنفُسَنَا وَإِن لَّمْ تَغْفِرْ لَنَا وَتَرْحَمْنَا لَنَكُونَنَّ مِنَ الْخَاسِرِين

Transliteration:

Rabbana ẓalamnā anfusanā wa in'l lam taghfir lanā wa-tarḥamnā lanu-kunan min al-khasirīn

Translation:

O Lord! We have wronged our own ourselves. If You do not forgive us and give us Your mercy, we will surely be lost.

Source: Surah Al-'Ārāf - 7:23

24. DU'A IN EMERGENCY TIMES

لا إله إلا الله العظيم الحليم؛ لا إله إلا الله رب العرش العظيم؛ لا إله إلا الله رب السموات، ورب الأرض، ورب العرش الكريم

Transliteration:

Lā ilaaha illa-allāhul-'āẓīm-ul al-ḥalīm, lā ilaaha illa-allāhu rabb-ul-'arshi'l-'āẓīm, Lā ilaaha illa-allāhu rabb us-samāwāti wa-rabb-ul-arḍi, wa rabb-ul-arsh'il-karīm.

Translation:

No one has the right to be worshipped except Allah, the Exalted, the Prudent. No one has the right to be worshipped except Allah, the Lord of the Mighty Throne. No one has the right to be worshipped except Allah, the Lord of the heavens and the Lord of the earth and the Lord of the honorable throne.

Source: Al-Bukhārī 634

25. DU'A FOR RIGHTEOUS CHILDREN

رَبَّنَا هَبْ لَنَا مِنْ أَزْوَاجِنَا وَذُرِّيَّاتِنَا قُرَّةَ أَعْيُنٍ وَاجْعَلْنَا لِلْمُتَّقِينَ إِمَامًا

Transliteration:

Rabbanā habb lanā min azwājinā wa-dhurīy-yātinā qurrata 'āyuūnin wa-j'alnā lil-muttaqīna imāman

Translation:

Our Lord! grant us delight in our spouses and our children, and make us a good example for the righteous.

Source: Surah Al-Furqān, 25:74

26. DU'A FOR CHILDLESSNESS AND LONELINESS

رَبِّ لَا تَذَرْنِيْ فَرْدًا وَّاَنْتَ خَيْرُ الْوٰرِثِيْنَ

Transliteration:

Rabbi lā tadharnī fardan wa anta Khaīr-ul Wārithīn

Translation:

O my Lord! Do not leave me alone (childless), though You are the best of heirs.

Source: Surah Al 'Anbīyā' 21:89

27. DU'A FOR PROTECTION FROM SATAN AND THE EVIL EYE (ENVY)

أُعِيـذُ نَفْسِي بِكَلِـماتِ اللهِ التَّـامَّة، مِنْ كُلِّ شَيْطانٍ وَهـامَّة، وَمِنْ كُلِّ عَيْنٍ لامَّـة

Transliteration:

'ūīdhu nafsī bi-kalimāt'il-allāhi-it-tāmmati min kulli shaīytānin wa-hāmmatin, wa-min kulli 'āīynin lāmmatin

Translation:

I seek refuge in the perfect words of Allah from every devil, from every poisonous thing, and from the evil eye that influences.

Source: Abu Dawūd 4737

28. DU'A FOR FORGIVENESS OF ALL SINS

اللَّهُمَّ اغْفِرْ لِي ذَنْبِي كُلَّهُ، دِقَّهُ وَجِلَّهُ، وَأَوَّلَهُ وَآخِرَهُ وَعَلَانِيَتَهُ وَسِرَّهُ

Transliteration:

Allāhumma aghfir lī dhanbī kulla-hu, diqqa-hu wajillahu, wa-awala-hu wa-ākhira-hu wa-ʿālānīyata-hu wa-sirrahu

Translation:

O Allah, forgive me all my sins, the great and the small, the first and the last, the obvious and the hidden.

Source: Abu Dawūd 878

29. DU'A FOR FORGIVENESS (TAUBA)

أَسْتَغْفِرُ اللهَ، أَسْتَغْفِرُ اللهَ، أَسْتَغْفِرُ اللهَ وَأَتُوبُ إِلَيْهِ

Transliteration:

Astagh-fi-rullāh, Astagh-fi-rullāh, Astagh-fi-rullāh, wa-atubu ilaīyhi

Translation:

I seek the forgiveness of Allah and repent with Him.

Source: Ṣaḥiḥ Muslim 1:414

30. DU'A FOR GUIDANCE AND PROTECTION

اللَّهُمَّ اغْفِرْ لِي، وَارْحَمْنِي، وَاهْدِنِي، وَاجْبُرْنِي، وَعَافِنِي، وَارْزُقْنِي، وَارْفَعْنِي

Transliteration:

Allāhumma aghfir lī, wa-arḥamnī, wa-hadinī, wa-jburnī, wa-'āfinī, wa-rzuqnī, wa-raf'anī

Translation:

O Allah forgive me, have mercy on me, guide me, support me, protect me, provide for me and uplift me.

Source: Sunan Ibn Mājah 3845, Jām'i at-Tirmidhī: 284

31. DU'A FOR MERCY

اللّهُمَّ إِنَّي أَسْأَلُكَ بِرَحْمَتِكَ الّتِي وَسِعَت كُلَّ شيء، أَنْ تَغْفِرَ لِي

Transliteration:

Allāhumma 'innī as-aluka bi-rahmatikal-latī wasi'at kulla shaīy'in an taghfira lī

Translation:

O Allah, I ask You by Your mercy, which encompasses everything, to forgive me.

Source: Ibn Mājah 1753

32. DU'A FOR ENTRY INTO PARADISE

رَبِّ ابْنِ لِي عِندَكَ بَيْتًا فِي الْجَنَّةِ

Transliteration:

Rabbi ibni lī 'indaka baīytan fi'l Jannati

Translation:

My Lord! Build a home for me with you in paradise.

Source: Surah At-Taḥrīm 66:11

33. DU'A FOR REPENTANCE

رَبِّ اغْفِرْ لي، وَتُبْ عَلَـيَّ، إِنَّكَ أَنْتَ التَّوّابُ الغَفُورُ

Transliteration:

Rabbi ighfir lī wa-tub 'alaīyya innaka anta-t-tawābu al-ghafūr

Translation:

My Lord, forgive me and accept my repentance, You are the All Forgiving, the All Merciful.

Source: Jām'i at-Tirmidhī 3434, Abu Dawūd 1516

34. DU'A FOR SUCCESS IN THIS WORLD AND BEYOND

رَبَّنَا آتِنَا فِي الدُّنْيَا حَسَنَةً وَ فِي الآخِرَةِ حَسَنَةً وَ قِنَا عَذَابَ النَّارِ

Transliteration:

Rabbanā Ātina fī al-dunīyā asanatan wa fī al-Ākhirati Ḥasanatan, wa-qinā 'Adhāba al-Nāri

Translation:

Our Lord, grant us what is goodness in this world and what is goodness in the Hereafter, and protect us from the torment of the fire.

Source: Surah Al-Baqarah 2:201

35. DU'A FOR A GOOD LIVELIHOOD

يا الله، يا رب، يا حيّ يا قيّوم، يا ذا الجلال و الإكرام، أسألك بأسمك العظيم الأعظم أن ترزقني رزقا واسعا حلالا طيّبا ، برحمتك يا أرحم الراحمين.

Transliteration:

Yā Allāh, yā Rabb, yā Ḥayy yā qywum, yā dhā al-Jalāl wa-al-ikrām, As'aluka bismika al-'Aẓīm al-A'ẓam an tarzuqany rizqan wās'an ḥlālan ṭyban, biraḥmatika yā arḥama alrāḥmyn.

Translation:

O Allah, O Lord, O Living, O Eternal, O Possessor of Majesty and Honor, I ask You by Your Great and Magnificent Name to grant me a generous, permissible and good sustenance, by Your Mercy, O the Most Merciful of the Merciful.

Source: Al-Bukhārī and Ṣaḥīḥ Muslim

36. DU'A TO TRUST IN ALLAH

رَبَّنَا آتِنَا مِن لَّدُنكَ رَحْمَةً وَهَيِّئْ لَنَا مِنْ أَمْرِنَا رَشَدًا

Transliteration:

Rabbanā ātinā mil-ladūnka raḥmatan wa-hayyī' lanā min amrina rashadā

Translation:

Our Lord! Have mercy upon us from You, and settle our matter for us in the right way!

Source: Surah Al-Kahf - 18:10

37. DU'A FOR FORGIVING

رَبَّنَآ أَمَنَّا فَاغْفِرْ لَنَا وَارْحَمْنَا وَأَنْتَ خَيْرُ الرّحِمِيْنَ

Transliteration:

Rabbanā āmannā faghfir lanā wa-rḥamnā wa anta khaīyrur rāḥimīn

Translation:

Our Lord! We believe, so forgive us and be merciful to us, for You are the best of all who have mercy.

Source: Surah Al-Mu'minūn 23:109

38. DU'A TO REPENTANCE

سُبْحَـانَكَ اللّهُـمَّ وَبِحَمدِك، أَشْهَدُ أَنْ لا إِلهَ إِلاَّ أَنْتَ أَسْتَغْفِرُكَ وَأَتوبُ إِلَيْك

Transliteration:

Subḥānāka Allāhumma wa bi-ḥamdika, Ash-hadu Ann
lā ilaha illā Anta, Astaghfiruka wa Atubu ilaīyka.

Translation:

The glory is Yours, O Allah, and the praise is Yours. I bear witness that there is none worthy of worship but Thee. I seek Your forgiveness and repent to You.

Source: Abu Dawūd 4859

39. DU'A FOR STRENGTHENING OF FAITH

رَبَّنَا لَا تُزِغْ قُلُوْبَنَا بَعْدَ اِذْ هَدَيْتَنَا وَهبْ لَنَا مِنْ لَّدُنْكَ رَحْمَةً اِنَّكَ اَنْتَ الْوَهَابُ

Transliteration:

Rabbanā Lā Tuzigh Qūlubānah Ba'da idh ḥadaīytānah wa-habb lanā mil-ladūnka raḥmatan innaka anta'l wahāb

Translation:

O Lord! Do not let our hearts deviate (from the truth) after You have guided us, and grant us mercy. Verily, You are the Beneficent.

Source: Surah Āl-'Imrān, 3:8

40. DU'A FOR GRATITUDE AND RIGHTEOUSNESS

رَبِّ أَوْزِعْنِي أَنْ أَشْكُرَ نِعْمَتَكَ الَّتِي أَنْعَمْتَ عَلَيَّ وَعَلَىٰ وَالِدَيَّ وَأَنْ أَعْمَلَ صَالِحًا تَرْضَاهُ وَأَدْخِلْنِي بِرَحْمَتِكَ فِي عِبَادِكَ الصَّالِحِينَ

Transliteration:

Rabbi āuwz'anī an ashkura ni'matikal-latī an'amta 'alaīyyah wa 'ala wālidaīyyah wa an 'āmala ṣāliḥān tarḍhāhu wa adkhilnī bi-raḥmatika fī 'ībādik aṣ-ṣāliḥīn

Translation:

My Lord, let me be grateful for Your favor shown to me and my parents, and be righteous. And by Your mercy, accept me into the ranks of Your righteous servants.

Source: Surah An-Naml, 27:19

41. DU'A FOR PROTECTION FROM SHIRK

اللّٰهُمَّ إِنِّي أَعوذُبِكَ أَنْ أُشْرِكَ بِكَ وَأَنا أَعْلَمُ، وَأَسْتَـغْفِرُكَ لِما لا أَعْلَم

Transliteration:

Allāhumma innī a'ūdhu bika an ūshrika bika wa-anā 'ālamu, wa-astaghfiruka limā lā 'ālamu

Translation:

O Allah, I seek refuge in You so that I may avoid all shirk, whether conscious or unconscious. And please forgive me for all my mistakes.

Source: Musnad Aḥmad 4:403

42. DU'A FOR MERCY AND FORGIVENESS

رَّبِّ اغْفِرْ وَارْحَمْ وَاَنْتَ خَيْرُ الرّحِمِيْنَ

Transliteration:

Rabbi ighfir wa-arḥam wa anta khaīyrur raḥimīna

Translation:

O Lord! Forgive and have mercy, for You are the best of those who grant mercy!

Source: Surah Al-Mu'minūn, 23:118

43. DU'A TO CONTROL ANGER

أَعُوذُ بِاللَّهِ مِنَ الشَّيْطانِ الرَّجِيْمِ

Transliteration:

A'ūdhu billāhi min ash-Shaīyṭāni ar-rajīm

Translation:

I seek refuge in Allah from Satan, the outcast.

Source: Abu Dawūd 4781, Al-Bukhārī 6115

44. DU'A FOR PROTECTION FROM STUPIDITY

اللّهُمَّ إِنِّي أَعُوذُ بِكَ أَنْ أَضِلَّ، أَوْ أُضَلَّ، أَوْ أَزِلَّ، أَوْ أُزَلَّ، أَوْ أَظْلِمَ، أَوْ
أُظْلَمَ، أَوْ أَجْهَلَ، أَوْ يُجْهَلَ عَلَيَّ

Transliteration:

Allāhumma innī a'ūdhu bika an aḍilla, auw ūḍalla, auw azilla, auw ūzalla, auw aẓlima, auw ūẓlama, auw ajhala auw yujhala 'alaīyya

Translation:

O Allah, I seek refuge in You lest I mislead others or be misled by others, lest I mislead others or be misled, lest I abuse others or be abused, and lest I act foolishly or meet the folly of others.

Source: Abu Dawūd 5094, Ibn Mājah 3884

45. DU'A AGAINST UNJUSTICE

عَلَى ٱللَّهِ تَوَكَّلْنَا ۚ رَبَّنَا ٱفْتَحْ بَيْنَنَا وَبَيْنَ قَوْمِنَا بِٱلْحَقِّ وَأَنتَ خَيْرُ ٱلْفَٰتِحِينَ

Transliteration:

Alallāhi tawakkalnā Rabbanā Aftaḥ Baīnanā Wa-Baīna Qawminā Bil-Ḥaqqi Wa Anta Khaīru Al-Fātiḥīna.

Translation:

In Allah is our trust. Our Lord! Decide thou between us and our people in truth, for thou art the best to decide.

Source: Surah Al-'Ārāf 7:89

46. DU'A AFTER EATING

الْحَمْدُ لِلَّهِ الَّذِي أَطْعَمَنِي هَذَا، وَرَزَقَنِيهِ مِنْ غَيْرِ حَوْلٍ مِنِّي وَلَا قُوَّةٍ

Transliteration:

Alḥamdu lillāhi-lladhī aṭ'amanī hadhā, wa-razaqanīhi min ghairi ḥauwlin minnī wa lā quwwah

Translation:

All praise is due to Allah, who has given me food to eat and provided it without my doing or strength.

Source: Jām'i at-Tirmidhī

47. DU'A FOR PEACE

اللَّهُمَّ أَنْتَ السَّلَامُ وَمِنْكَ السَّلَامُ، تَبَارَكْتَ يَا ذَا الْجَلَالِ وَالإِكْرَامِ

Transliteration:

Allāhumma Antas-Salām wa minkas-salām. Tabārakta yā Zal-jalāli wal- ikrām.

Translation:

O Allah, You are As-Salam (Peace), From You is all peace, blessed are You O Possessor of majesty and honour.

Source: Ṣaḥiḥ Muslim 592

48. DU'A FOR ASSISTANCE AND SUPPORT

يَاحَيُّ، يَا قَيُّومُ، بِرَحْمَتِكَ أَسْتَغِيثُ، أَصْلِحْ لِي شَأْنِي كُلَّهُ، وَلَا تَكِلْنِي إِلَى نَفْسِي طَرْفَةَ عَيْنٍ

Transliteration:

Yā Ḥayyu yā Qayyūm, bi raḥmatika astaghīthu, aṣliḥ lī sha'nī kullahu, wa lā takilanī ila nafsī Ṭarfata 'Aīaynin.

Translation:

O Ever-Living, O Self-Subsisting and Supporter of all, in Your mercy I seek relief. Rectify my affairs, all of them, and do not entrust me to myself even for the blink of an eye.

Source: Ṣaḥīḥ at-Targhīb wat-Tarhīb 1:273

49. DU'A FOR JUSTICE

رَّبِّ اغْفِرْ لِي وَلِوَالِدَيَّ وَلِمَن دَخَلَ بَيْتِيَ مُؤْمِنًا وَلِلْمُؤْمِنِينَ وَالْمُؤْمِنَاتِ وَلَا تَزِدِ الظَّالِمِينَ إِلَّا تَبَارًا

Transliteration:

Rabbi-ighfirlī wali-wāli-dayya wa-liman dakhala baīytīa mu'minan wa-lil-mu'minīna wal-mu'mināt walā tazidi aẓ-ẓālīmīna illā tabarān

Translation:

My Lord, forgive me and my parents and him who enters my house believing, and the believing men and the believing women; but plunge the unrighteous all the more deeply into destruction.

Source: Surah Nūḥ, 71:28

50. DU'A FOR EXAM PREPARATION

اللهم افتح لي أبواب حكمتك، وانشر عليّ رحمتك، وامنن علي بالحفظ والفهم، سبحانك لا علم لنا إلا ما علمتنا، إنك أنت العليم الحكيم

Transliteration:

Allāhumma aftaḥ lī abwāb ḥikmatika, wa-nshur 'alaīya raḥmataka, wa-amnin 'alaīyun bil-ḥifz wal-fahmu, subḥānakā lā 'ilm lanā ilaa mā 'alimatanā, inaka anta al-'alīm al-ḥakīmu.

Translation:

O Allah, open the doors of Your wisdom to me, spread Your mercy over me and grant me learning and understanding, glory be to You. We have no knowledge except what You have taught us, for You are the All-Knowing, the Wise.

Source: Ṣaḥiḥ Muslim

51. DU'A FOR MOTIVATION

رَبِّ أَوْزِعْنِى أَنْ أَشْكُرَ نِعْمَتَكَ ٱلَّتِى أَنْعَمْتَ عَلَىَّ وَعَلَىٰ وَٰلِدَىَّ وَأَنْ أَعْمَلَ صَٰلِحًا تَرْضَٰهُ

وَأَصْلِحْ لِى فِى ذُرِّيَّتِىٓ إِنِّى تُبْتُ إِلَيْكَ وَإِنِّى مِنَ ٱلْمُسْلِمِينَ

Transliteration:

Rabbi āuwz'inī an ashkura ni'matikal-latī an'amta 'alaīyyah wa 'ala wālidaīyyah wa an 'āmala ṣāliḥan tarḍhāhu wa-aṣliḥ lī fī dhūrīyatī innī tūbtu ilāīyka wa-innī min al-muslimīna

Translation:

My Lord, inspire me to be grateful for Your mercy shown to me and my parents, and (inspire me) work righteousness that may please You. And let my offspring be righteous to me. Verily, I have repented to Thee, and verily, I am one of the Muslims.

Source: Surah Al-Aḥqāf, 46:15

52. DU'A FOR FORGIVENESS

انْتَ وَلِيُّنَا فَاغْفِرْ لَنَا وَارْحَمْنَا وَأَنْتَ خَيْرُ الْغَافِرِينَ وَاكْتُبْ لَنَا فِي هٰذِهِ الدُّنْيَا حَسَنَةً وَفِي الْآخِرَةِ إِنَّا هُدْنَا إِلَيْكَ

Transliteration:

Anta walīyyūnā faghfir lanā wa-rḥamnā wa anta khaīr ul-ghāfirīna waktūb lanā fī hadhi hid-dunyā ḥasanatan wafi al-ākhirati innā hudnā ilaīyka

Translation:

Lord, You are our protector; so forgive us and have mercy on us; for You are the best of the forgiving. Decree good for us, both in this world and in the hereafter; for to You we have returned repentant.

Source: Surah Al-A'raf - 7:155-156

53. DU'A FOR PATIENCE

رَبَّنَا أَفْرِغْ عَلَيْنَا صَبْراً وَثَبِّتْ أَقْدَامَنَا وَانصُرْنَا عَلَى القَوْمِ الكَافِرِينَ

Transliteration:

Rabbanā Afrigh 'Alaīynā Ṣabrān Wa-Thabbit Aqdāmanā Wa-Anṣurnā 'Ala Al-Qawmi Al-Kāfirīna.

Translation:

Our Lord, pour down patience on us, and strengthen our foothold, and support us against the faithless people.

Source: Al-Baqarah 2:250

54. DU'A FOR PROTECTION AGAINST MISERY AND ENEMIES

اللهمَّ إِنِّي أَعُوذُ بِكَ مِنْ جَهْدِ الْبَلَاءِ، وَدَرَكِ الشَّقَاءِ، وَسُوءِ الْقَضَاءِ، وَشَمَاتَةِ الْأَعْدَاءِ

Transliteration:

Allāhumma 'innī a'ūthu bika min jahdi albalā'i, wa daraki ash-shaqāi, wa sū'i alqadā'i, wa shamātati al'adā'i.

Translation:

O Allah, I beseech You to protect me from hardship, misfortune, bad fortune and the gloating of my enemies.

Source: al-Bukhārī 6347; Ṣaḥiḥ Muslim

55. DU'A FOR EXAM SUCCESS

رَبِّ أَدْخِلْنِي مُدْخَلَ صِدْقٍ وَأَخْرِجْنِي مُخْرَجَ صِدْقٍ وَاجْعَلْ لِي مِنْ لَدُنْكَ سُلْطَانًا نَصِيرًا

Transliteration:

Rabi adkhilnī mudkhal ṣidqin wa-akhrijnī mukhraj ṣidqin wa-j'al lī min ladūnka sulṭānan naṣīran

Translation:

O my Lord, let my entrance be a good entrance and let my exit be a good exit. And grant me Your helpful power.

Source: Surah Al-Isrā, 17:80

56. DU'A FOR THE SUPPORT OF ALLAH

رَبَّنَا لَا تُؤَاخِذْنَا إِن نَّسِينَا أَوْ أَخْطَأْنَا ۚ رَبَّنَا وَلَا تَحْمِلْ عَلَيْنَا إِصْرًا كَمَا حَمَلْتَهُ عَلَى الَّذِينَ مِن قَبْلِنَا ۚ رَبَّنَا وَلَا تُحَمِّلْنَا مَا لَا طَاقَةَ لَنَا بِهِ ۖ وَاعْفُ عَنَّا وَاغْفِرْ لَنَا وَارْحَمْنَا ۚ أَنتَ مَوْلَانَا فَانصُرْنَا عَلَى الْقَوْمِ الْكَافِرِينَ

Transliteration:

Rabbanā lā tu-akhidnā in-nasīnā auw akhṭ'anā rabbanā wa lā taḥmil 'alaīynā iṣrān kamā ḥamaltahu 'ala-al-ladhīna min qablinā rabbanā wa lā tūḥammilnā mā lā ṭāqata lanā bihi wa-'fu 'annā wa-ghfirlanā wa-rḥamnā anta mauwlānā fa-nṣurnā 'ala'l qauwm'il al-kāfirīna

Translation:

Our Lord, do not reproach us if we forget (something) or commit mistakes. O Lord, do not put a burden on us as You put it on those who were before us. O Lord, do not burden us with anything for which we have no strength. And forgive us and have mercy on us. You are our protector. So help us against the people of the unbelievers!

Source: Surah Al-Baqarah, 2:286

57. DU'A AT SINS

اللَّهُمَّ إِنَّكَ عَفُوٌّ كَرِيمٌ تُحِبُّ الْعَفْوَ فَاعْفُ عَنِّي

Transliteration:

Allāhumma innaka 'afuwwun karīmun tuḥibbul 'afwa' fā'fu 'annī

Translation:

O Allah, You are truly forgiving, [generous,] You appreciate forgiveness, so please forgive me.

Source: Jām'i at-Tirmidhī 3513

58. DU'A TO PRAISE ALLAH

الْحَمْدُ لِلَّهِ حَمْدًا كَثِيرًا طَيِّبًا مُبَارَكًا فِيهِ غَيْرَ مُوَدَّعٍ وَلاَ مُسْتَغْنًى عَنْهُ رَبُّنَا

Transliteration:

Alḥamdulillāhi ḥamdan kathīran ṭaīyybān mūbarakān fīhi, ghaīra muwadda'in wa lā mustaghnan 'anhu Rabbūnā

Translation:

All praise is due to Allah - abundant, pure and blessed praise; praise that can neither be dispensed with nor omitted, O Lord.

Source: Jām'i at-Tirmidhī

59. DU'A FOR SPIRITUAL MOTIVATION

اللَّهُمَّ أَعِنِّي عَلَى ذِكْرِكَ، وَشُكْرِكَ، وَحُسْنِ عِبَادَتِكَ

Transliteration:

Allāhumma 'āinnī 'ala dhikrika, wa-shukrika, wa-ḥusni 'ibādatika

Translation:

O Allah, help me to always remember You, be grateful to You and worship You in an excellent way.

Source: Abu Dawūd Book 16, Ḥadīth 1422

60. DU'A AGAINST ENVY AND EVIL EYE

بسم الله أرقي نفسي, من كلّ شيء يؤذيني, من شر كلّ نفس أو عين حاسد, الله يشفيني ,بسم الله أرقي نفسي

Transliteration:

Bismallāhi arqī nafsī, min kulli shaī'in yu'dhīnī, min sharri kulli nafsin auw 'aynīn ḥāsid, Allāhu yashfīnī, Bismallāhi arqī nafsī.

Translation:

O Allah, I pray to you to purify me from all sorrows, from every harmful evil, and from the evil of the eyes of an envious person.

Source: Ṣaḥīḥ Muslim

61. DU'A FOR LOVE

اللَّهُمَّ إِنِّي أَسْأَلُكَ فِعْلَ الْخَيْرَاتِ، وَتَرْكَ الْمُنْكَرَاتِ، وَحُبَّ الْمَسَاكِينِ، وَأَنْ تَغْفِرَ لِي، وَتَرْحَمَنِي، وَإِذَا أَرَدْتَ فِتْنَةَ قَوْمٍ فَتَوَفَّنِي غَيْرَ مَفْتُونٍ، وَأَسْأَلُكَ حُبَّكَ وَحُبَّ مَنْ يُحِبُّكَ، وَحُبَّ عَمَلٍ يُقَرِّبُنِي إِلَى حُبِّكَ.

Transliteration:

Allāhumma innī As-aluka fi'la al-khaīrāt wa Tarka al-munkarāt wa-Ḥubba al-masākīn wa-an-taghfira lī wa-Tarḥamanī. Wa-idha arad-ta fitnata qawmin fa-tawaffanī ghaīyra maftun. Wa as-aluka Ḥubbaka wa-Ḥubba man yuḥibbuka wa-Ḥubba 'amalin yuqarribunī ila Ḥubbika.

Translation:

O Allah! I ask of you the doing of the good deeds, avoiding the evil deeds, loving the poor, and that You forgive me, and have mercy upon me. And when You have willed Fitnah in the people, then take me without the Fitnah. And I ask You for Your love, the love of whomever You love, and the love of the deeds that bring one nearer to Your love.

Source: Jām'i at-Tirmidhī 5/369

62. DU'A FOR HEALING

اللهمّ رَبَّ النَّاسِ أَذْهِبِ البَاسَ، واشْفِ أَنْتَ الشَّافِي، لا شِفَاءَ إِلَّا شِفَاؤُكَ، شِفَاءً لا يُغَادِرُ سَقَمًا.

Transliteration:

Allāhumma rabba an-nās adhhib al-b'as, washfi anta al-ashāfī, lā shifā'a illa shifā'uka, shifā'an lā yughādiru saqaman.

Translation:

O Allah, Lord of mankind, take away the pain, and heal, You are the Healer, there is no cure but Your healing, a cure that does not leave sickness.

Source: Al-Bukhārī with Al-Fatḥ 10/206 and Ṣaḥiḥ Muslim 4/1721

63. DU'A IN DEBT AND DEPRESSION

اللّهُمَّ إِنِّي أَعْوذ بِكَ مِنَ الهَمِّ وَ الْحُـزْنِ، والعَجْـزِ والكَسَلِ والبُخْـلِ والجُـبْنِ وضَلْـعِ الـدَّيْنِ وغَلَبَـةِ الرّجال

Transliteration:

Allāhumma innī a'ūdhu bika min al-hammi wal-ḥuzni, wal-ajzi wal-kassali, wal-būkhli wal-jūbni, wa-ḍali' al-dīni wa ar- ghalabati rijāli

Translation:

O Allah, I seek refuge in You from sorrow and sadness, from weakness and laziness, from stinginess and cowardice, from being overwhelmed by debt and from being overwhelmed by other people.

Source: Al-Bukhārī 7/158; Al-'Asqalānī, Fatḥul-Bārī 11/173

64. DU'A FOR PROTECTION IN CASE OF UNKNOWN EVENTS AND PERSONS

اللّهُـمَّ إِنِّـي أَسْـأَلُكَ خَيْـرَها، وَأَعـوذُ بِكَ مِنْ شَرِّها

Transliteration:

Allāhumma innī as-aluka khaīrahā, wa a'ūdhu bika min sharrihā

Translation:

O Allah, I ask You for the good in it and seek refuge in You from its evil.

Source: Abu Dawūd 5084, Ibn Mājah 2252

65. DU'A FOR A SUCCESSFUL DAY

أَصْبَحْنَا وَأَصْبَحَ الْمُلْكُ لِلَّهِ رَبِّ الْعَالَمِينَ، اللَّهُمَّ إِنِّي أَسْأَلُكَ خَيْرَ هَذَا الْيَوْمِ، فَتْحَهُ، وَنَصْرَهُ، وَنُورَهُ وَبَرَكَتَهُ، وَهُدَاهُ، وَأَعُوذُ بِكَ مِنْ شَرِّ مَا فِيهِ وَشَرِّ مَا بَعْدَهُ.

Transliteration:

Aṣbaḥnā wa-aṣbaḥ al-mūlku lillāhi rabb'il-'ālamīn, Allāhumma innī as-aluka khaīra hadha-al-yauma, fatḥahu, wa-naṣrahu, wa-nūrahu, wa-barakatahu, wa-hudāhu, wa-a'ūdhu bika min sharri mā fīhi, wa-sharri mā ba'dahu.

Translation:

We have reached the morning, and at this time all sovereignty belongs to Allah, the Lord of the Worlds. O Allah, I ask You for the good of this day, its triumphs and its victories, its light and its blessings and its guidance, and I take refuge in You from the evil of this day and the evil that follows it.

Source: Abu Dawūd 4:322

66. DU'A FOR PROTECTION FROM EVIL

أَعُوذُ بِكَلِمَاتِ اللَّهِ التَّامَّاتِ مِنْ شَرِّ مَا خَلَقَ.

Transliteration:

A'ūdhu bi-kalimāt-illāh it-tāmmati min sharri mā khalak

Translation:

I take refuge in Allah's perfect words from the evil He has created.

Source: Musnad Aḥmad 2:290, Jām'i at-Tirmidhī 3:187

67. DU'A FOR DESPAIR

رَبِّ إِنِّي لِمَا أَنزَلْتَ إِلَيَّ مِنْ خَيْرٍ فَقِيرٌ

Transliteration:

Rabbi innī limā anzalta ilaīyya min khaīyrin faqīrun.

Translation:

My Lord! I am in (desperate) need of all the good that You send down for me.

Source: Surah Al-Qaṣaṣ 28:24

68. DU'A FOR PROTECTION DURING SLEEP

اَمْسَيْنَا وَ اَمْسَ الْمُلْكُ لِلَّهِ وَالْحَمْدُ لِلَّهِ، لَا إِلَهَ إِلَّا اللهُ وَحْدَهُ لَا شَرِيكَ لَهُ، لَهُ الْمُلْكُ وَلَهُ الْحَمْدُ وَهُوَ عَلَى كُلِّ شَيْءٍ قَدِيرٌ، رَبِّ أَسْأَلُكَ خَيْرَ مَا فِيْ هَذِهِ اللَّيْلَةِ وَخَيْرَ مَا بَعْدَهَا، وَأَعُوْذُ بِكَ مِنْ شَرِّ مَا فِي هَذِهِ اللَّيْلَةِ وَشَرِّ ما بعدها، رَبِّ أَعُوْذُ بِكَ مِنَ الْكَسَلِ، وَسُوءِ الْكِبَرِ، رَبِّ أَعُوْذُ بِكَ مِنْ عَذَابٍ فِيْ النَّارِ وَعَذَابٍ فِيْ الْقَبْرِ.

Transliteration:

Amsaīnā wa-amsal mulku lillāh wal-ḥamdu lillāh, lā ilaha illā allāhu, wa-aḥdahu lā sharīka lahu, lahu al-mūlku wa lahu al-ḥamd, wahu wa 'ala kulli shaī'yin qadīr, rabbi as-aluka khaīra mā fī hadhi hil-laīylah, wa-khaīra mā ba'dahā, wa-a'ūdhu bika min sharri hadhi hil-laīyla, wa-sharri mā ba'dahā, rabbi a'ūdhu bika min al-kasal, wa-sū'il kibar, rabbi a 'ūdhu bika min 'adhābi fī-nār, wa 'adhāb-in fī'l-qabr.

Translation:

We and the entire kingdom of Allah have reached the evening and all sovereignty and all praise is due to Allah. No one has the right to be worshipped except Allah alone. To Him belongs all sovereignty and all praise, and He is omnipotent over everything. Lord, I ask You for the good of this night and the good that follows it, I seek protection from You from laziness and confusion. Lord, I look to You for protection from the punishment of fire and the torment of the grave.

Source: Ṣaḥiḥ Muslim 4:2088

69. DU'A FOR GRATITUDE

اللَّهُمَّ مَا أَمْسَ بِي مِنْ نِعْمَةٍ أَوْ بِأَحَدٍ مِنْ خَلْقِكَ فَمِنْكَ وَحْدَكَ لَا شَرِيكَ لَكَ، فَلَكَ الْحَمْدُ وَلَكَ الشُّكْرُ.

Transliteration:

Allāhumma mā amsa bī min ni'matin, auw bi-aḥadin min khalqika, fa-minka wa-ḥdaka lā sharīka laka, fa-la kal-ḥamdu wa laka sh-shūkr.

Translation:

O Allah, whatever blessing has come to me or to any of Your creatures is from You alone. Thus, all praise is due to You and all thanks are due to You.

Source: Abū Dawūd 4:318

70. DU'A FOR CONTENTMENT IN LIFE

رَضِيتُ بِاللَّهِ رَبَّا، وَبِالْإِسْلَامِ دِيناً، وَبِمُحَمَّدٍ صَلَى اللَّهُ عَلِيهِ وَسَلَّمَ نَبِيَّاً

Transliteration:

Raḍitu billāhi rabban wa-bil-islāmi dīnān wa-bi-Muḥammadin (Ṣallal-lahuʿalaīhi Wasallama) nabīyyan.

Translation:

I am satisfied with Allah as Lord and Islam as religion and Muḥammad (Ṣallal-lahuʿalaīhi Wasallama) as its prophet.

Source: Abu Dawūd 4:318

71. DU'A FOR ANY WORLDLY STRESS AND UNHAPPINESS

أَن لَّآ إِلَهَ إِلَّآ أَنتَ سُبحَـٰنَكَ إِنِّى كنتُ مِنَ ٱلظَّـٰلِمِينَ

Transliteration:

An Lā ilāha illa Anta Subḥānaka innī Kuntu Mina Aẓ-Ẓālimīna

Translation:

There is no god except You. Glory be to You! I was one of the Wrongdoers.

Source: Surah Al 'Anbīyā' 21:87

72. DU'A FOR PAIN AND ILLNESS

اللَّهُمَّ لك الحمد وإليك المشتكى وأنت المستعان و بك المستغاث و عليك التكلان ولا حول ولا قوّة ألاّ بك.

Transliteration:

Allāhumma laka al-hamdu wa ilayka al-mashtaka wa anta al-musta'aan wa bika al-mustaghaas wa 'alayka al-taklaan wa-lā ḥawla wa-lā qūwata illā bika.

Translation:

O Allah, all praise is for You, and to You is the complaint; You are the One Who helps and with You is the hope for aid; upon You is to rely and there is no power and no strength except through You.

Source: Ibn Taimiya

73. DU'A IN THE FEARS

بِسْمِ اللَّهِ الَّذِي لَا يَضُرُّ مَعَ اسْمِهِ شَيْءٌ فِي الْأَرْضِ وَلَا فِي السَّمَاءِ وَهُوَ السَّمِيعُ الْعَلِيمُ

Transliteration:

Bismallāhi al-ladhī lā yaḍūrru ma'a-asmihi shaīy'un fī'l-arḍi wa lā fī as-samā'i wa hua as-samī'i-ul-'alīm.

Translation:

In the name of Allah, by whose name nothing is harmed on earth or in the heavens. He is the All-Seeing, the All-Knowing.

Source: Abu Dawūd 4:323

74. DU'A IN PAIN

أَعُوذُ بِعِزَّةِ اللَّهِ وَقُدْرَتِهِ مِنْ شَرِّ مَا أَجِدُ وَأُحَاذِرُ

Transliteration:

A'ūdhu bi'izzatillāhi wa-qudratihi min sharri mā ajidu wa-ūḥādhiru

Translation:

I seek refuge in Allah and in His power from the evil that afflicts me and from what I fear.

Source: Ṣaḥīḥ Muslim

75. DU'A IN UNHAPPINESS

رَبِّي أَنِّي مَسَّنِيَ الضُّرُّ وَأَنْتَ أَرْحَمُ الرَّاحِمِينَ

Transliteration:

Rabbī annī massanī aḍ-ḍurru wa anta arḥamu-r ar-rāḥimīna

Translation:

My Lord. Truly, misfortune has touched me, and You are the most merciful of the merciful.

Source: Surah Al 'Anbīyā' 21:83

76. DU'A FOR HEALING

رَبَّنَا اللَّهُ الَّذِي فِي السَّمَاءِ تَقَدَّسَ اسْمُكَ أَمْرُكَ فِي السَّمَاءِ وَالأَرْضِ كَمَا رَحْمَتُكَ فِي السَّمَاءِ فَاجْعَلْ رَحْمَتَكَ فِي الأَرْضِ اغْفِرْ لَنَا حُوبَنَا وَخَطَايَانَا أَنْتَ رَبُّ الطَّيِّبِينَ أَنْزِلْ رَحْمَةً مِنْ رَحْمَتِكَ وَشِفَاءً مِنْ شِفَائِكَ عَلَى هَذَا الْوَجَعِ فَيَبْرَأُ

Transliteration:

Rabbanā Allāhul-ladhī fī as-samāʻi taqaddasas-ismūka amrūka fī as-samāʻi wa'l-arḍi kamā raḥmatuka fī as-samāʻi fa-j'al raḥmataka fī'l-arḍi. ighfir lanā ḥūbanā wa-khaṭāyānā anta rabb-uṭ-ṭayyībīn anzil raḥmatan min raḥmatika wa-shifā'an min shifā'ika 'ala hadha'al waja'ī fa-yabra'ū

Translation:

O our Lord, Allah who is in heaven, holy be Your name, Your will be done in heaven and on earth; as Your mercy is in heaven, bestow it on earth. Forgive us our sins and our wrong ways. You are the Lord of good. Send down mercy from You and remedies from You to heal this pain, so that it may be healed.

Source: Abū Dāwūd

77. DU'A FOR PROTECTION AGAINST UNDERHANDEDNESS

اللَّهُمَّ احْفَظْنِي مِنْ بَينِ يَدَيَّ ,وَمِنْ خَلْفِي ,وَعَنْ يَمِينِي ,وَعَنْ شِمَالِي وَمِنْ فَوْقِي ,وَأَعُوذُ بِعَظَمَتِكَ أَن أُغْتَالَ مِنْ تَحْتِي

Transliteration:

Allāhumma aḥ-faẓnī min baīni yadaīya, wa-min khalfī, wa-'an yamīnī, wa-'an shimālī wa-min fawuqī, wa-a'ūdhu bi-'aẓmātika an ughtāla min taḥtī.

Translation:

O Allah, protect me from the front, from the back, from the right and from the left and from above, and I seek refuge in Your glory, lest I be assaulted from below.

Source: Sunan Ibn Mājah

78. DU'A FOR PROTECTION FROM SATAN (DEVIL)

رَّبِّ أَعُوذُ بِكَ مِن هَمَزَاتِ ٱلشَّيَـٰطِينِ وَأَعُوذُ بِكَ رَبِّ أَن يَحضُرُونِ

Transliteration:

Rabbi a'ūdhu-bika min hamazāt as-shaīyātīn waa-a'ūdhu bika rabi an yaḥḍurūn.

Translation:

O Lord! I seek refuge in You from the whispers of Shaitan (devil). And I seek refuge in You, my Lord, so that they do not come near me.

Source: Surah Al-Mu'minūn 23:97-98

79. DU'A FOR PROTECTION OF PHYSICAL AND MENTAL HEALTH

اللَّهُمَّ إِنِّي أَعُوذُ بِكَ مِنَ الْبَرَصِ، وَالْجُنُونِ، وَالْجُذَامِ، وَمِنْ سَيِّئِ الْأَسْقَامِ

Transliteration:

Allāhumma innī a'ūdhu-bika min-al baraṣi, wal-jūnūni wal-jūdhām, wa-min saīyyī'il-asqām

Translation:

O Allah, I seek refuge in You from leprosy, madness, elephantiasis and evil diseases.

Source: Abū Dawūd

80. DU'A FOR RIGHTEOUS CHILDREN

رَبِّ هَبْ لِي مِنَ الصَّالِحِينَ

Transliteration:

Rabbi hab lī min aṣ-ṣāliḥīna

Translation:

My Lord! Bless me with righteous descendants.

Source: Surah As-Ṣaffāt, 37:100

81. DU'A FOR LEARNING AND EDUCATION

رَبِّ زِدنِي عِلمًا

Transliteration:

Rabbi zidnī 'ilmā.

Translation:

O Allah, increase my knowledge!

Source: Surah Ṭaha, 20:114

82. DU'A FOR A PURE SOUL

اللَّهُمَّ إِنِّي أَعُوذُ بِكَ مِنْ عِلْمٍ لاَ يَنْفَعُ ,وَمِنْ دُعَاءٍ لاَ يُسْمَعُ ,وَمَنْ قَلْبٍ لاَ يَخْشَعُ ,وَمِنْ نَفْسٍ لاَ تَشْبَعُ

Transliteration:

Allāhumma innī a'ūdhu-bika min 'ilmin lā yanfa'ū, wa-min du'ā-in lā yusma'ū, wa-min qalbin lā yakhsha'ū, wa-min nafsin lā tashba'ū.

Translation:

O Allah, I seek refuge in You from a knowledge that is of no use, from a supplication that is not answered, from a heart that does not fear (You), and from a soul that is never satisfied.

Source: Sunan Ibn Mājah

83. DU'A FOR SUPPLY (RIZQ)

اَللَّهُمَّ رَبَّنَآ أَنزِلْ عَلَيْنَا مَآئِدَةً مِّنَ ٱلسَّمَآءِ تَكُونُ لَنَا عِيدًا لِّأَوَّلِنَا وَءَاخِرِنَا وَءَايَةً مِّنكَ ۖ وَٱرْزُقْنَا وَأَنتَ خَيْرُ ٱلرَّزِقِينَ

Transliteration:

Allāhumma rabbana anzil ʿalaynā māʾidatam minas-samāʾi takūnu lanā ʿīdan li-awwalinā wa-ākhirinā wa-āyatan minka wa-arzuqnā wa-anta khayrur-raẓiqīn.

Translation:

O Allah our Lord! Send us from heaven a table set (with viands), that there may be for us— for the first and the last of us a solemn festival and a sign from Thee; and provide for our sustenance, for Thou art the best Sustainer (of our needs).

Source: Surah Al-Maeda 5:114

84. DU'A FOR MAKING THE RIGHT DECISIONS

رَبَّنَا آتِنَا مِن لَّدُنكَ رَحْمَةً وَهَيِّئْ لَنَا مِنْ أَمْرِنَا رَشَدًا

Transliteration:

Rabbanā ātinā mil-ladūnka raḥmatan wa-hayyī' lanā min amrina rashadā

Translation:

Our Lord, grant us Your mercy and prepare a way for our cause.

Source: Surah Al-Kahf, 18:10

85. DU'A FOR A SUCCESSFUL STUDY

اَللَّهُمَّ انْفَعْنِي بِمَا عَلَّمْتَنِي وَعَلِّمْنِي مَا يَنْفَعُنِي وَزِدْنِي عِلْمًا

Transliteration:

Allāhuma anfa'nī bimā 'allamtanī, wa 'allimnī mā yanfa'unī, wa-zidnī 'ilmā

Translation:

O Allah! Grant me benefit in what you have taught me, and teach me useful knowledge and increase my knowledge.

Source: Jām'i at-Tirmidhī

86. DU'A FOR EXAMINATIONS

اللَّهُمَّ لَا سَهْلَ إلاَّ مَا جَعَلْتَهُ سَهْلاً، وأَنْتَ تَجْعَلُ الحَزْنَ إذَا شِئْتَ سَهْلاً

Transliteration:

Allāhumma lā sahla illā mā ja'altahu sahlān, wa-anta taj'al ul-ḥazna idhā shi'ta sahlā.

Translation:

O Allah! Nothing is easy except what You have made easy. If You want, You can make the difficult easy.

Source: Ṣaḥīḥ Ibn Ḥibbān

87. DU'A TO ACHIEVE A GOOD CHARACTER

اللَّهُمَّ إِنِّي أَعُوذُ بِكَ مِنْ مُنْكَرَاتِ الأَخْلاَقِ، وَالأَعْمَالِ، وَالأَهْوَاءِ

Transliteration:

Allāhumma innī a'ūdhu-bika min munkarāt-il akhlāq, wal-'āmāl, wal-ahwa'

Translation:

O Allah! I seek refuge in You from undesirable behavior, deeds and goals.

Source: Jām'i at-Tirmidhī

88. DU'A FOR BUSINESS SUCCESS

اللَّهُمَّ إِنِّي أَسْأَلُكَ عِلْمًا نَافِعًا وَرِزْقًا طَيِّبًا وَعَمَلاً مُتَقَبَّلاً

Transliteration:

Allāhumma innī as-aluka 'ilmān nāfi'an, wa-rizqan ṭayyīban, wa-'amalan mutaqabbalan

Translation:

O Allah, I ask You for useful knowledge, good provision and good deeds.

Source: Sunan Ibn Mājah 925

89. DU'A FOR ALLAH'S SUPPORT

رَبِّ أَعِنِّي وَلَا تُعِنْ عَلَيَّ، وَانْصُرْنِي وَلَا تَنْصُرْ عَلَيَّ، وَامْكُرْ لِي وَلَا تَمْكُرْ عَلَيَّ، وَاهْدِنِي وَيَسِّرِ الْهُدَى إِلَيَّ، وَانْصُرْنِي عَلَى مَنْ بَغَى عَلَيَّ

Transliteration:

Rabbi 'Āinnī wa lā tu'in 'alayya, wan-Ṣurnī wa-lā tanṣur 'alayya, wam-kūr-lī wa-lā tamkur 'alayya, wahdinī wa-yassiri-l al-Huda' ilaīyya, wan-Ṣurnī 'ala man Bagha 'alayya.

Translation:

My Lord, help me and do not give help against me; grant me victory, and do not grant victory over me; plan on my behalf and do not plan against me; guide me, and made my right guidance easy for me; grant me victory over those who act wrongfully towards me.

Source: Jām'i at-Tirmidhī

90. DU'A FOR SUCCESSFUL FUTURE

رَبِّي هَبْ لِي حُكْماً و أَلْحِقْنِي بِالصَّالِحِينَ، وَاجْعَل لِي لِسَانَ صِدْقٍ فِي الآخِرِينَ، وَ اجْعَلْنِي مِنْ وَرَثَةِ جَنَّةِ النَّعِيم

Transliteration:

Rabbi hab lī ḥukmān wa-alḥiqnī biṣāliḥīna wa aj'al lī lisāna ṣidqin fī-al-'ākhirīna wa-aj'alnī min-warathati jannati an-na'īm

Translation:

My Lord, grant me wisdom and make me one of the righteous. Bless me with honorable mention among the later generations and make me one of the heirs of the Garden of Bliss.

Source: Surah Ash-Shū'ara, 26:83-85

91. DU'A FOR A GOOD FAMILY AND A SUCCESSFUL MARRIAGE

رَبَّنَا هَبْ لَنَا مِنْ أَزْوَٰجِنَا وَذُرِّيَّٰتِنَا قُرَّةَ أَعْيُنٍ وَٱجْعَلْنَا لِلْمُتَّقِينَ إِمَامًا

Transliteration:

Rabbanā habb lanā min azwājinā wa-dhurīy-yātinā qurrata 'āyuūnin wa-j'alnā lil-muttaqīna imāman.

Translation:

Our Lord! Bless us with spouses and offspring who are the joy of our hearts, and make us examples for the righteous.

Source: Surah Al Fūrqān, 25:74

92. DU'A FOR SUCCESS AND VICTORY IN LIFE

اللهُمَّ اجْعَلْنَا مُفْلِحِينَ

Transliteration:

Allāhumma a-ja'alnā mūfliḥīna

Translation:

O Allah, make us successful people.

Source: Sunan An-Nasā'ī

93. DU'A FOR SUCCESSFUL LIVING

اللَّهُمَّ اجْعَل خَيْرَ عُمُرِي آخِرُهُ و خَيْرَ عَمَلِي خَوَاتِمَهُ وَ اجْعَلْ خَيْرَ أَيَّامِي يَوْمَ أَلْقَاكَ

Transliteration:

Allāhumma ja'al khaīyra 'ūmrī ākhirahu wa-khaīyra 'amalī khawātimahu wa-j'al Khaīra ayyāmī yauma alqāka

Translation:

O Allah, make the best part of my life the last part, the best deed my last deed, and the best day the day I meet You.

Source: Sunan An-Nasā'ī

94. DU'A WITH REPENTANCE

رَبَّنَآ اِنَّنَآ اٰمَنَّا فَاغْفِرْ لَنَا ذُنُوْبَنَا وَقِنَا عَذَابَ النَّارِ

Transliteration:

Rabbanā innanā āmannā fa-aghfir lanā dhūnubanā wa-qinnā 'adhāb an-nār

Translation:

O Lord! We have truly believed, so forgive us our sins and save us from the punishment of fire.

Source: Surah Āli-'Imrān, 3:16

95. DU'A AFTER WUDU (ABLUTION BEFORE PRAYER)

اللَّهُمَّ اجْعَلْنِي مِنَ التَّوَّابِينَ وَاجْعَلْنِي مِنَ الْمُتَطَهِّرِينَ

Transliteration:

Allāhumma aj'alnī mina at-tawwābīna wāj'alnī mina al-mūtaṭahirīna.

Translation:

O Allah! Make me those who repent and those who purify themselves.

Source: Jami' At-Tirmidhī

96. DU'A FOR THE REPENTANT

رَبَّنَا وَسِعْتَ كُلَّ شَيْءٍ رَّحْمَةً وَعِلْمًا فَاغْفِرْ لِلَّذِينَ تَابُوا وَاتَّبَعُوا سَبِيلَكَ وَقِهِمْ عَذَابَ الْجَحِيمِ

Transliteration:

Rabbana wasi'at kulla shai'in r-raḥmatan wa-'ilmān faghfir lil-ladhīna tābū wat-taba'ū sabīlaka wa-qihim 'adhāb al-Jaḥīm

Translation:

Our Lord, You have encompassed everything in mercy and knowledge; so forgive those who repent and follow Your path, and protect them from the agony of the Blaze.

Source: Surah Ghāfir - 40:7

97. DU'A BEFORE SLEEP

بِاسْمِكَ رَبِّي وَضَعْتُ جَنْبِي، وَبِكَ أَرْفَعُهُ، فَإِنْ أَمْسَكْتَ نَفْسِي فَارْحَمْهَا، وَإِنْ أَرْسَلْتَهَا فَاحْفَظْهَا، بِمَا تَحْفَظُ بِهِ عِبَادَكَ الصَّالِحِينَ.

Transliteration:

Bismika rabbī waḍ'atu janbī wa-bika arfa'ūhu, fā-in amsakta nafsī far-ḥamhā, wa-in arsaltahā fa-ḥfaẓhā bi-mā taḥfaẓu bi-hi 'ībādaka aṣ-ṣaliḥīn

Translation:

In Your name, my Lord, I lie down, and in Your name I rise. If You should take my soul, have mercy on it, and if You should return my soul, protect it as You do Your righteous servants.

Source: Al-Bukhārī 11:126

98. DU'A FOR GUIDANCE AND CONTENTMENT

اللَّهُمَّ إِنِّي أَسْأَلُكَ الْهُدَى، وَالتُّقَى، وَالْعَفَافَ، وَالْغِنَى

Transliteration:

Allāhumma innī As-aluka al-huda' waltuqa', wal 'Afāfa wal-Ghina'

Translation:

O Allah! I ask You for guidance, piety, chastity and contentment.

Source: Ṣaḥīḥ Muslim

99. DU'A FOR A DECEASED

اللهُمَّ اغْفِرْ لِـفُلَانٍ (باسمه) وَارْفَعْ دَرَجَتَهُ فِي المَهْدِيّينَ وَاخْلُفْهُ فِي عَقِبِهِ فِي الغَابِرِينَ، وَاغْفِرْ لَنَا وَلَهُ يا رَبَّ العَالَمِـينَ، وَافْسَحْ لَهُ فِي قَبْـرِهِ وَنَـوِّرْ لَهُ فِيهِ

Transliteration:

Allāhumma aghfir li-fulān warfa' darajatahu fīl-mahdiyyīna, wakhlūfhu fī 'aqibihi fī al-ghābirīna, wa-aghfir-lanā wa-lahu yā Rabb al-'ālamīna, wa-fasaḥ lahu fī qabrihi wa-nawwir lahu fīhi

Translation:

O Allah, forgive [person's name] and elevate his position among the righteous. Send him in the way of those who came before him, and forgive us and him, O Lord of the Worlds. Enlarge for him his grave and let light fall upon him therein.

Source: Ṣaḥīḥ Muslim 2:634

AUDIO BONUS

For beginners of Arabic, it is advisable to learn the correct stress and articulation of the du'as from a native speaker. On my YouTube channel "99 Duas" you will find 10 consecutive Du'as each in Fus'ha Arabic (modern standard Arabic). They begin with "Subhanallah" and end with "Salat Ibrahimiya".

https://cutt.ly/99duas-de-us

Have fun and Allah's blessings!

IMPRINT

Author: Salah Moujahed

Publisher: BAAB Publishing

Cover Design: Eagles Media Design

Editing: Hassan Mehmood

Print: Amazon

c/o BAAB Ltd

59 Mere Road ; B23 7LL Birmingham; United Kingdom

salah@muslimnotebooks.com

Copyright© Salah Moujahed